MW01712724

Steven Curtis Chapman

THE MUSIC OF CHRISTMAS

ISBN 0-7935-5737-2

HAL•LEONARD™ CORPORATION

7777 W. BLUEMOUND RD. P.O. BOX 13819 MILWAUKEE, WI 53213

HARK! THE HERALD ANGELS SING

Words by CHARLES WESLEY
Music by STEVEN CURTIS CHAPMAN

C/E G/D C G/B Am E/G♯ Am D/F♯ G
of the skies; — with the an - gel - ic host pro - claim Christ is — born in
C D/F♯ G C G/B Am E/G♯ Am D/F♯ G
Beth - le - hem! Hark! the her - ald an - gels sing glo - ry — to the
Csus2 Am E
new - born King.
F♯m/E C♯m7

A(add2)
B/A
F♯m7
E
A(add2)
1
2
E
There's _ a
man
who
la - dy _
who
fire, ______
tell the
A(add2)
E
F♯m7
E/G♯
3
stands in the cold wind to - night
and he greets ev - 'ry - one pass - in'
sits all a - lone with her thoughts
and the mem-'ries of all that she's
fam - 'ly to gath - er a - round
and the walls _ will ech - o the

A(add2)
F#m7
E
by
with a smile and a ring - in' bell.
lost
when she hears a sound at her door.
sound
of mem - 'ries that are and will be.
3
A(add2)
And the song that he's play-in' is his
And the song comes to find her as a
And their voic - es like a cho - rus will
E/G#
A
F#m7
E
own way of say - in'
gen - tle re - mind - er
sing it so sweet - ly for us,
love is here,
B7sus
E
1
A(add2)
it's the mu - sic of Christ - mas.
And there's a

2,3
Asus2
E
So listen, listen with your heart
C♯m7
and you will hear a
G♯m7
song in the
A
A/B
laughter of a child.
E
A(add2)
3
Oh, won't you
E
listen
for the sound of
C♯m
hope,
you will hear the

G#m7
A
G#m7
To Coda
A
B
mu - sic of Christ-mas, for the mu - sic of Christ - mas is love.
E
Asus2
D.S. al Coda
(take 2nd ending)
Oh, it's love. So, light a
CODA
A
B
Asus2
C#m
Christ - mas is love.
F#m7
E/G#

Asus2
E
Long _ a - go a
A
E
F#m7
E/G#
ba - by was born in the night.
And as He let out His ver - y first
Asus2
F#m7
E
cry,
the sound was bring-ing hope a - live. _
Stars were
A(add2)
E/G#
shin-in', an - gels sing - in', __ all heav'n and earth was ring -

A F♯m7 E B7sus
- in', love is here. This is the mu - sic of
3
A E
Christ - mas. So, lis - ten, lis - ten with your heart
C♯m7 G♯m7
and you will hear a song in the
A A/B E Asus2 E
laugh - ter of a child. Oh, come on and lis - ten

C♯m
for the sound _ of hope, _
you will hear _ the
G♯m7
A
G♯m7
A
mu - sic,
mu - sic,
G♯m7
3
A B
E
for the mu-sic of Christ - mas _ is love. _
3
Asus2
E
Lis - ten, _

A(add2)
E
A
Lis - ten with _ your heart. _
3
3
E
You'll hear the mu - sic, ___ lis - ten. _
A(add2)
A E/G♯ F♯m7
E/G♯ A B
E5

CHRISTMAS IS ALL IN THE HEART

Words and Music by
STEVEN CURTIS CHAPMAN

C/G
Am7/D
- lie Brown's. And un - der-neath there's one lit - tle gift for
of dawn with Mom and Dad and cam - 'ras mak - in'
D7
G
him, and one lit - tle gift for her.
sure we'd nev - er for - get that day.
C/G
G
C/G
G
Af - ter six months on the new
Now I'm the one who's tak - in' pic -
C/G
G
C/G
G
job, they're still bare - ly get - tin' by. So, in the way of dec - o - ra -
- tures in the mid - dle of the night of my own blonde-head - ed

C/G
G
- tions, there's noth - in' there _ to catch _ your eye. _ And
dream - ers who just can't wait _ un - til _ day - light. _ And
Am7/D
both of them _ would be the first _ to say
in my sleep - y eyes the spark _ still glows,
Am7
G/B
we're to - geth - er, and we're gon - na have _ the mer - ri - est Christ -
I guess there's just some things _ a kid _ nev - er _
Am7/D
G
- mas an - y - way. _
out - grows. _
'Cause Christ - mas _ is all _

D/G
in the heart, that's where the feel - ing starts
Dm/F
E7
Am
and like a fire in - side, it
G/B
touch - es ev - 'ry part, 'cause Christ - mas is all
Am7/D
G
in the heart. And e - ven if

D/G
no white snow falls,
that's { al - right, / o - kay, } be - cause
Dm/F
E
Am
the joy can still be found wher -
G/B
- ev - er you are 'cause Christ - mas is all,
Am7/D
1
G
C/G
all in the heart.

G
C/G
2
G
Two lit - tle
No, it's
C
G/B
Am7
D♯dim7
not in the snow that may or may not fall.
Em
C
G/B
Am7
D♯dim7
And it's not in the gifts a - round the tree.
Em
C
G/B
Am7
It's in the love heav - en gave the

D#dim7
Em
D
C
night our Sav - ior came. And that same Love can still be found
G/B
Csus2
wher - ev - er you are 'cause
3
Am
B/D#
Em
Christ - mas is all in the heart. And the joy
E7
Am
can still be found wher - ev - er you are

G/B
Am7/D
'cause Christ - mas is all,
all in the heart.
G
C/G
G
C/G
G
It's all in the heart.
C/G
G
C/G
G
rit.

ANGELS WE HAVE HEARD ON HIGH

Words by EDWARD BARNES
Music by STEVEN CURTIS CHAPMAN

Bm A A/C♯ D
ech - o at their joy - ous strains.
C♯/E♯ F♯m E/G♯ A
Glo - ri - a, glo - ri - a.
A D/F♯ E/G♯
Shep - herds, why this ju - bi - lee?
Come to Beth - le - hem and see
Bm A A/C♯ D
Why your joy - ous strains pro - long?
Him whose birth the an - gels sing;
A D/F♯ E/G♯
Say what may these tid - ings be
come a - dore on bend - ed knee

Bm
A
A/C♯
D
which in - spire _ your heav - en - ly song? _
Christ, the Lord, _ the new - born King.
C♯/E♯
F♯m
E/G♯
A
Glo - ri - a, _ glo - ri - a.
Em/G
F♯7
Glo. . .
Bm
Dm/F
A/E
D
B/D♯

A/E E A/E E F♯m E/G♯ A Bm A E/G♯
glo - ri - a in ex - cel - sis De - o,
Em/G F♯7 Dm/F Dm
glo. . .
A/C♯ D B/D♯ A/E E A/E E
glo - ri - a
F♯m E/G♯ A Bm/D
1
A/E E A D/F♯ E/G♯
in ex - cel - sis De - o.

Bm
A
A/C♯
D
2
A/E
E
3
D
E/D
De - o.
F♯m
E/F♯
F♯m
Dmaj7
E/D
Dsus2

Bm
A/C#
D
F#m
no chord
Em/G
F#7
Glo. . .
Bm
Dm/F
A/E
D
B/D#

A/E E Esus E F♯m E/G♯ A Bm B♭ F
glo - ri - a ___ in ex - cel - sis De - o.
Fm/A♭ G7 E♭m/G♭ E♭m
Glo. . .
B♭/D E♭ C/E B♭/F F
glo - ri - a ___
Gm F/A B♭ Cm B♭ F/A Fm/A♭
in ex - cel - sis De - o, in ex - cel - sis

G7sus
G7
E♭m/G♭
E♭m
De - o, in ex - cel - sis
B♭/F
F
B♭
E♭/G F/A
De - o.
Cm
B♭
B♭/D
E♭
B♭
E♭/G F/A
Cm
B♭
B♭/D
E♭
Repeat and Fade

O COME, O COME EMMANUEL

Words Translated by JOHN M. NEALE and HENRY S. COFFIN
Music by STEVEN CURTIS CHAPMAN

F(add2) Am Em/G F C/E
ad - vent here; dis - perse the gloom - y clouds of night,
Dm7 C/E F/G G C
and death's dark shad-ows put to flight. Re - joice! Re -
Am B♭ F/A Dm7 C/E
joice! Em - man - u - el shall come to thee, O
F F/G G7 C Am B♭
Is - ra - el! Re - joice! Re - joice! Em - man - u -

F/A
Dm7
C/E
F
F/G
G7
Am
Em7
el shall come to thee, O Is - ra - el! Re - joice!
Am
Em7
F
C/E
E♭
D♭/F
G♭dim7
Oh, re -
D♭
B♭m
C♭
joice! Re - joice! Em - man - u -

Gb/Bb Gb Db/F Ebm7 Db/F Gb Gb/Ab Ab7 Db
el shall come to thee, O Is - ra - el! Re - joice! Re -
Bbm Cb Gb/Bb Gb Db/F Ebm7 Db/F
joice! Em - man - u - el shall come to thee, O
Gb Gb/Ab F7/A Bbm Ab Gb Db/F Ebm7 Db/F Gb Gb/Ab
Is - ra - el! Re - joice! Re-joice! Em-man - u - el shall come to thee! Re -
Db Fm Bbm Fm/Ab Gb Gb/Ab Db
joice!

OUR GOD IS WITH US

Words and Music by STEVEN CURTIS CHAPMAN
and MICHAEL W. SMITH

Bbm7
Gbsus2
One of us is cry - in' as our hopes and dreams are lead a - way in
spoke through pro - phets' voic - es and showed Him - self in a cloud of
Db
Absus
chains and we're left all a - lone. And
fire. No one had seen His face un -
Bbm7
Gbsus2
one of us is dy - in' as our love is slow - ly low - ered in the grave,
til the one most ho - ly re - vealed to us His per - fect heart's de - sire
Db
Absus
oh, and we're left on our own. But for
and left His right - ful place. And

Bbm7
Ab(add9)/C
all of us who jour - ney through the dark a - byss of
in one glo - rious mo - ment all e - ter - ni - ty was
Gb
3
Absus
lone - li - ness, there comes a great an-nounce - ment: we are nev - er a - lone.
shak - en as God broke through the dark - ness that had kept us a - part.
Ab
Gb
For the mak - er of each heart that breaks, the
And with love that con - quers lone - li - ness, the
Ab
Gb/Bb
Giv - er of each breath we take, has come to earth and giv - en
hope that fills all emp - ti - ness, He came to earth to

Ab/C
Absus
Ebm/Db
Db
hope its birth.
show our way.
And our God is with us,
Db/F
Gb
Em - man - u - el.
Ebm/Bb
Bbm
He's come to save us,
Abm7
Em - man - u - el.

Abm7/Db
Db7/F
Cb/Gb
Gb
And we will nev - er
F7sus
F7/A
Bbm
face life a - lone now that God has
Ab
Eb/G
Ebm
made Him - self known as Fa - ther and friend with
Gbm6/A
To Coda
Db
us through the end, Em - man - u - el.

Ab/C
Bbm
Oh.
Gbsus2
Absus
Db
Gb/Bb
Absus
Ab
D.S. al Coda
He
CODA
Bbm
Ab/C
Db
Ebm
Db/F
Ab
So, re - joice,

B♭m A♭/C B♭m
oh, re - joice.
A♭/C B♭m/D♭ E♭m F/A
Em - man - u -
B♭m A♭/C D♭ D♭/F G♭
el has come.
F♯/E Em/D D
And our God is with us,

D/F#
G
Em - man - u - el.
Em6/B Bm
He's come to save us,
Am7
Em - man - u - el.
D7/F#
G
And we will never

F♯7sus F♯7 Bm
face life ___ a - lone ___ now that God has
Bm/A E/G♯ Em
made him - self known ___ as Fa - ther _ and friend, with
A7sus F♯/A♯ Bm Bm/A
us to the end, Em - man - u - el. ___
E/G♯ Em Gm6/B♭
Our God _ is with ___ us,

D
D/F♯
Em - man - u - el.
G
Bm
Asus A
Our God _ is
Em/D
D
D/F♯
with us,
G
Gm6/B♭
Gm6
Repeat and Fade
oh, Em - man - u - el.

INTERLUDE: THE MUSIC OF CHRISTMAS

Arranged by STEVEN CURTIS CHAPMAN
and ROBIE BUCHANAN

D/F♯
Bm F♯m/A G A/G D/F♯ D/G G D/A
Am
G/F
F/E♭
D D/F♯ G
D/A Bm G D/A
E/A
C/A
B/A
rit.
Slower
Em/G B/D♯ Em B7/F♯ Em/G E/G♯ A A/G

(𝅗𝅥 = ♩)
D/F# G D/A Am7
D G/D G/D G/D D
F#m G D/F# G D/F# G A7/E
D D/A A7 D A7 D F#m G
D/F# Bm F#m/A G D/F# G A7/E D/F# D/A A7 D A7
D Bm F#m G Em7 F#sus F#7/A# Bm F#m/A G

D/F♯ G A7/E D/F♯ D/A A♯dim7 Bm D/A G D/F♯
B♭/F D A/C♯ G D/F♯ G A7 D/F♯ D/A Am7 D
rit.
Moderately, with motion
no chord

D B Em A D G/B
Em A7 D/F♯ Em/G D/A G/B D/A A7sus A7 D B
Em A7 D G/B Em A7 D/F♯ Em/G D/A G/B
Much faster
D/A F/A
A/C♯ B/D♯ Em Asus
3
3
no chord
3

G
E/G♯
A
D
D/A
D/G
B♭/F
E♭
B♭/D
B♭
B♭/F
E♭
B♭/D
D/C
G/B
B/D♯
Em
C
rit.
G/D
A7/D
D
Dsus
G5

THIS BABY

Words and Music by
STEVEN CURTIS CHAPMAN

2
B♭ C F
Well, he cried when he was hun - gry, did
- by grew in - to a young boy. He learned to
B♭ C F B♭ C Dm
all the things that ba - bies do. He rocked and he napped on his
read and write and wres - tle with Dad. There was the climb - ing of trees and the
B♭
3
moth - er's lap and he wig - gled and wig - gled and cooed. There were the
scrape of knees and all the fun that a boy's born to have. He grew
C F B♭ C F
cheers when he took his first step and the tears when he got his first
tall - er and some things start - ed chang - ing, like his com - plex - ion and the sound of his

B♭ C Dm
teeth. Al - most ev - 'ry - thing a - bout this lit - tle
voice. There was the work to be done as a
B♭ B♭sus2
ba - by seemed as nat - u - ral as it could be.
car - pen - ter's son, and all the neigh - bors said he's such a fine boy.
C F B♭ C
But this (1., D.S.) ba - by boy made the an - gels sing, and this ba - by boy made a
F B♭ C F F/A Dm
new star shine in the sky. This ba - by boy had come to change the world.

B♭ F C Dm
This ba - by / boy was God's own Son.
B♭ F C Dm B♭ F C
This ba - by / boy was like no oth - er one. This ba - by / boy was God
Dm To Coda B♭sus2
with us. This ba - by was Je - sus.
1
3

2
B♭sus2
Dm
And this ba - This boy be - came a man. Love
B♭
G7/B
made him laugh, death made him cry, but the life that He lived and the death
F/C
A7/C♯
Dm
3
that He died, He showed us heav - en with His hands and His heart
B♭
F/A
C
Dm
'cause this man was God's own Son.
And this man was like

Am7 Dm
Bb F/A
C
no oth - er one; ho - ly and pure right from the
Dm
D.S. al Coda
CODA
Bb
start, yeah, yeah.
This ba - by,
F F/A
this ba - by was Je - sus.
Bbsus2
Repeat and Fade
This ba - by was Je -

SILENT NIGHT, HOLY NIGHT • AWAY IN A MANGER • O HOLY NIGHT

"SILENT NIGHT, HOLY NIGHT"
Words by JOSEPH MOHR
Music by FRANZ GRÜBER

Arranged by
STEVEN CURTIS CHAPMAN

Moderately slow

F Dm7 Em Am
Ho - ly in - fant so ten - der and mild,
Dm G7 G♯dim Am7 D9/F♯
sleep in heav - en - ly peace,
C/G G7 Am7 G/B C Em
sleep in heav - en - ly peace.
"AWAY IN A MANGER"
Words by MARTIN LUTHER
Music by JONATHAN E. SPILLMAN
Am7 G/B C Em D/F♯ G
A - way in a
near me, Lord

Em7 C G/B Am7
man - ger, no crib for a bed, the lit - tle Lord
Je - sus, I ask thee to stay close by me for -
D/F# C Bm7 Am7 G
Je - sus laid down His sweet head. The stars in the
ev - er and love me I pray. Bless all the dear
Em7 C G/B Am D/F#
sky looked down where He lay, the lit - tle Lord
chil - dren in thy ten - der care and fit us for
Em7 1 Am D/F# G
Je - sus a - sleep on the hay.
heav - en to
1

C
2
Am7
G/B
C
Be
live
with
Thee
Em
there.
Am7
Fmaj9
Esus
D/A
A
G/A
D

"O HOLY NIGHT"
English Words by D.S. DWIGHT
Music by ADOLPHE ADAM

F♯m/C♯ C♯7 F♯m
peared, and the soul felt its worth. A
G/A A7 D
thrill of hope the wear - y world re - joic - es, for
G/A A7 D A/C♯
yon - der breaks a new and glo - rious morn!
Bm F♯m
Fall on your knees! O

Em
Bm
Gm/B♭
hear the an - gel voic - es! O
D/A
A7
A♯dim
Bm
G
night di - vine! O
D/A
A7
D
D/F♯
night when Christ was born! O
A7
A♯dim
Bm
Bm/A
G
Gm6
night di - vine, O

D
1
A7
D
A/C♯
night,
O night di - vine!
2
A7
D
O night di - vine!
G
D
G
Em
Gm6/B♭
D
rit.

CAROL OF THE BELLS

UKRANIAN
Arranged by STEVEN CURTIS CHAPMAN

B
Em
B
Em
Em/D
Em/C
Em/B
Em/C
Em/B
Em/A
Em/B
Em
D/E
Em
D/E
Em
To Coda
1

2
Am/E
Em
Am/E

Em
B
Em/B
B
Em/B
Em
Em/D
Em/C
Em/B
Em/C
Em/B
Em/A
Em/B
Em
D.S. al Coda
CODA
D/E
Em
no chord

O COME ALL YE FAITHFUL

Words and Music by JOHN FRANCIS WADE
Latin Translation by FREDERICK OAKELEY
Arranged by STEVEN CURTIS CHAPMAN

D A/C# E F#m B/D#
and tri - umph - ant, O come ye O
ex - al - ta - tion, O sing, all ye
E A/E E B
come ye to Beth - le -
cit - i - zens of heav'n a -
E Esus E A/F# E/G# A D
hem; Come and be -
bove; Glo - ry to
Word of the
Bm C# C#7 F#m7 B7
hold him, born the King of
God, all glo - ry in the
Fa - ther now in flesh ap -

Bm7 D/E A E/A A D/E
an - gels;
high - est;
pear - ing;
O come, let us a -
A E/A A D/E A
dore Him, O come, let us a - dore
E/G# A D A/C# Bm C# F#m D
Him, O come, let us a - dore Him,
A/E E To Coda A E/A A D/A
1
A
Christ the Lord.

E/A A D/A A
E/A A E
2
A D/B A/C♯ D E
Oh, For He a - lone is
D/A A C♯ C♯7 C♯7/E♯ F♯m
worth - y, for he a - lone is worth -
D Bm C♯ C♯7 F♯m D
y. O come, let us a - dore him,

A/E E A
the Lord.
Christ Come and let us a -
D E A D
dore Him, come and let us a - dore
E F♯m C♯7/E♯
Him. Yea, Lord, we bless thee,
A/E B7/D♯ D
born for our sal - va - tion; O Je -

E C♯m A/C♯ F♯m A/B B7
sus, for - ev - er be Thy Name a -
D/E E D.S. al Coda
dored.
CODA
F♯m7 D/F♯ A/E Esus
Lord.
D Dmaj7 A2/C♯ A/C♯ D Bm C♯ C♯7
O come, let us a - dore
F♯m D A/E E
Him, Christ, oh, Christ

E7sus
A
D
E
the Lord.
Come and let us a - dore Him,
F♯m
D
E
A
come and let us a - dore Him. Come and
D
E
F♯m
let us a - dore Him, come and let us a -
Play three times
D
E
G(add9)
Asus2
dore Him.

GOING HOME FOR CHRISTMAS

Words and Music by STEVEN CURTIS CHAPMAN
and JAMES ISAAC ELLIOT

E D A
- ble and gifts were placed be - neath the tree.
where they could watch her night and day.
and gifts and grand - pa comes a - lone.
D
Ev - 'ry - thing was pic - ture per - fect. Grand -
But she kept mak - ing plans for Christ - mas
There's a sad - ness in our si - lence as the
A/C♯ D
pa would laugh - and say, "That wom - an spends the whole
from her lit - tle room. She told ev - 'ry - one, "I'll miss
Christ - mas sto - ry's read. And with tears, grand-pa re - minds
A/C♯ Bm Esus7
year get - tin' read - y for this day."
you, but I'll be leav - ing soon."
us of the words that grand - ma said.

1
2
E
E A/C♯ D
One
I'm go - in' home
A
for Christ - mas
and I'm
go - in' home to stay.
D
I'm go - in' home for Christ -
A/E

E
Esus
D
E
- mas
and noth-in's gon-na keep me a-way.
A
D
A/C#
D
D/E
And I'll be
(D.S.) And she'll be
A
A/C#
with the ones I love to cel-e-brate the Sav-ior's birth.
face to face with Je-sus as we cel-e-brate His birth.
D
A/C#
This gift will be worth more to me than
(her)

Bm
A/C♯
D
an - y - thing on earth.
I'm go - in'
'cause she'll be
home,
E7sus
To Coda
E
A
home for Christ - mas.
3
F♯m7
3

D.S. al Coda
(take 2nd ending)
D
Dsus2
3
All the
CODA
E
Em/G
And as we sing "Joy To The World" I can't help think-
F♯sus
F♯
Bm
-in' of the joy that's shin - ing in
A/C♯
D
her eyes right now.
And

Em/G
D/F♯
though our hearts still ache, we know that as we cel - e - brate,
Bm
A/C♯
she's sing - in' with the her - ald an - gels and heav - en's
D
E7sus
glow - in' on her face.
E
A/C♯
D
A
And now she's home for Christ -

D
- mas, oh, now she's home to stay.
A/E
Oh, she's home for Christ -
E Esus D E
- mas; noth - ing could - 've kept her a - way.
A D A/C♯ D D/E
Yeah, she'll be

A
A(add2)/C♯
face to face with Je - sus as we cel - e - brate His birth.
D
A/C♯
And His gift will be worth more to her than an -
Bm
A/C♯
D
- y - thing on earth. She's home,
E7sus
E
A
she's home for Christ - mas.

F#m7
D
And she is home,
E7sus
E
A
she's home for Christ - mas.
E
D
A
F#m7
E/D
D
A
rit.

PRECIOUS PROMISE

Words and Music by
STEVEN CURTIS CHAPMAN

G
C
G
she's gon - na have _ a son.
And though it's a pre - cious prom -
Oh, what a pre - cious prom -
D/F#
Em7
Bm7
- ise, ___ she won - ders how can __ this be? ___
- ise, ___ oh, what a gift __ of love. ___
C
D
G
What will the peo - ple say ___ and __ what if Jo - seph can't __ be - lieve? _
Jo - seph _ makes _ his choice _ to ___ do what few men would have done: ___
The wait - ing now __ is o - ver and __ the time has fin - 'lly come _
Am7
And her ques - tions and ___ her fears __
to take Ma - ry as ____ his bride _
for the God who made __ this world _

Am7(♭5)
are met with an
when she's al - read - y car -
to roll back the cur -
G
D/F♯
o - ver-whelm - ing joy that God has chos - en her.
- ry - ing a child that is - n't his own.
- tain and un - veil His pas - sion for the heart of
Em7
C
man.
Oh, what a pre - cious prom -
D/C
Am7
To Coda
D
- ise;
Ma - ry waits as heav - en comes to
Ma - ry and the child will have a
ly - ing in a

1
G
D/F♯
Em7
earth.
D/C
C
2
G
home.
D/F♯
Em7
And shep - herds _ stand on ___ a
Bm7
C
hill - side, __ their _ hearts rac - ing with __ the news _

D
C G
the angel told them. A
Em7
Bm7
star's light fills up the dark sky
C
G/B
as the night of precious promise is unfolding.
C
D.S. al Coda
CODA
D
D♯dim
manger in Bethlehem.

Em7
C
Oh, what a pre - cious prom -
Am7
D
- ise ly - ing in a man - ger in Beth - le -
G
D/F♯
Em7
hem.
C(add2)
G5